TRIFOLD
MIRROR

POETIC REFLECTIONS ON THE
ONE WHO SAVED ME

TRIFOLD
MIRROR

POETIC REFLECTIONS ON THE
ONE WHO SAVED ME

CHIDIEBERE EZE
Illustrated by Ana P. Guerra

GOD MANIFEST PUBLISHING
www.godmanifestpublishing.com

This book and all other God Manifest Publishing books are available on Amazon.com.

Cover designed by Chidiebere Eze and Jonnathan Zin Truong
Illustrations by Ana P. Guerra
Interior designed by Jonnathan Zin Truong

For more information on foreign distributors, email
publishers@godmanifestpublishing.com

ISBN: 979-8-9857412-7-8
eBook: ISBN: 979-8-9857412-8-5

DEDICATION

To my family and friends who stayed close,
yet distant enough, which quickened my desire
for an intimate relationship with God.

TABLE OF CONTENTS

THE HOOD

Dear reader,

This collection is a piece of my heart
And I'm delighted to share it with you
I hope you enjoy reading it as much as I have loved creating it

As you work through the pages
I encourage you to meditate on what is laid on your heart
Utilize the spaces of reflection provided at the end of the book
To document your revelations as God unveils Himself to you

May the Holy Spirit speak to you

All my love,

Chichi

Introduction

My dear Father

The Hero of our universe

I've decided to write about You

(Like a book is enough to describe Your thousand-plus sides)

I hope my depiction of what we share

Captures a glimpse of how You make me feel

That with You, love will always come first

Fried Plantain

Someone tried explaining to me
How boiled plantains taste better than deep-fried plantains

I couldn't bring myself to argue
All I asked was, *"Have you tried fried plantains?"*
Because that was all I wanted to know

In the same light
How can one argue that God doesn't exist
When they haven't offered to "try" Him?
There are just not enough words
To explain how good He tastes

A person doesn't argue about what they are convinced of
They show proof

Let me show you my God

*"O taste and see that the Lord [our God] is good; How
blessed [fortunate, prosperous, and favored by God] is
the man who takes refuge in Him." Psalm 34:8, AMP*

Seek

From a now-believer of Christ
to someone else, perhaps struggling to believe

He graciously revealed Himself to me
So, don't be scared to ask Him to unveil Himself

He is a showoff
So, allow Him to make you His centerpiece

He is a spender
So, allow Him to lavish you with His extravagance

He is a jealous lover
So, allow Him to soak you with His affection

If you've found Him
Consider yourself favored

If you haven't found Him yet, seek Him until you do
Through the study of His Word and prayer

*"All that My Father gives Me will come to Me; and the one who
comes to Me I will most certainly not cast out [I will never,
never, reject anyone who follows Me]." John 6:37, AMP*

Charge

Some days feel harder than others

Like You are not in control

Like demons are having a field day

No profits for smart and hard hustlers

No returns for long-time investors

No harvest for diligent farmers

But are You ever not in control?

Creation emerged from nothing at Your command

The Great Flood dried up at Your decree

The Red Sea parted at the force of Your word

Some days feel like You are not in control

Not because You aren't

But because I'm too blinded by worries to see

That as King, Your greatest weapon is Your Word

Whatever You say must come to pass

And if it hasn't yet come to pass

Then it is not the end

Because You are the End

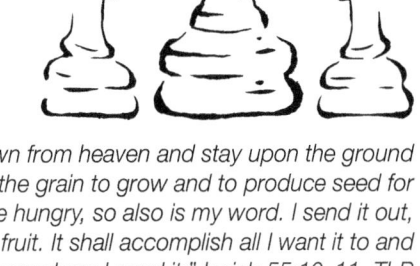

"As the rain and snow come down from heaven and stay upon the ground to water the earth, and cause the grain to grow and to produce seed for the farmer and bread for the hungry, so also is my word. I send it out, and it always produces fruit. It shall accomplish all I want it to and prosper everywhere I send it." Isaiah 55:10–11, TLB

Limitless

I tried to put Him in a box

so He broke the box

Tried to limit Him in my goals and dreams

so He blew my imagination

Tried to honor preset boundaries between us

so He tore the separating veil of holies

Nailed Him to a cross to kill Him

so He defeated death

Confined Him to a grave

and He resurrected

What exactly can hold Him down?

A boundless and limitless God

How did we ever become worthy

To be called one of His?

"He wraps the waters in His clouds [which otherwise would spill on earth all at once], and the cloud does not burst under them. He covers the face of the full moon and spreads His cloud over it. He has inscribed a circular limit (the horizon) on the face of the waters at the boundary between light and darkness. The pillars of the heavens tremble and are terrified at His rebuke. He stirred up the sea by His power, and by His understanding He smashed [proud] Rahab. By His breath the heavens are cleared; His hand has pierced the [swiftly] fleeing serpent. Yet these are just the fringes of His ways [mere samples of His power], The faintest whisper of His voice! Who can contemplate the thunder of His [full] mighty power?" Job 26:8–14, AMP

What About Me?

He blessed a generation with Abraham

Walked with Noah

Rescued a nation with Moses

Delivered salvation for humanity through Mary

Restored mankind to Himself with Jesus

Ever wonder if He'll choose you?

Yeah? Me too

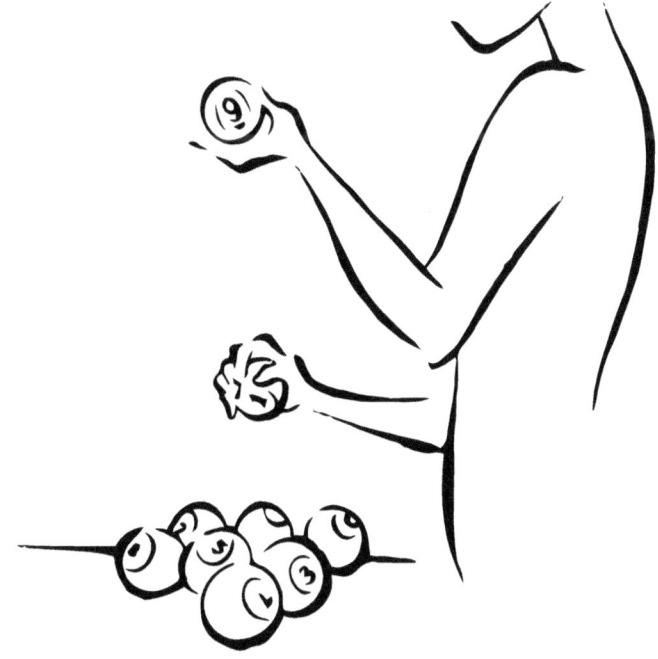

"And those whom He predestined, He also called; and those whom He called, He also justified [declared free of the guilt of sin]; and those whom He justified, He also glorified [raising them to a heavenly dignity]." Romans 8:30, AMP

Equal

I learned not to be envious

Not of the way He loves the offender as much as He does the offended

Not of the way He loves the sinner as much as He does the righteous

Because He made it clear from the beginning of time

That He would leave the ninety-nine

And come after the lost one

I whispered under my breath

Judging the attention-seeking "one"

Especially in moments when I waited with the other ninety-eight

Until He asked me, *"What makes you think you are part of the ninety-nine?"*

So, what exactly am I?

Then I prayed to be the one

The one I had subconsciously judged

At least then, I'll be assured He'll come after me

"I tell you, in the same way there will be more joy in heaven over one sinner who repents than over ninety-nine righteous people who have no need of repentance." Luke 15:7, AMP

One with Him

I had heard of His power
But not physically felt it
I thought people exaggerated
Sometimes I doubted it was true
Tasty tales enveloped with lies
All because I hadn't felt Him for myself

But He wanted me to know Him
He needed me to believe Him
He desired for me to experience Him

So, He came for me
With what felt like a heated, rushing wind
Determined, strong, and true
I surrendered
My hands in His
His Spirit in mine
My body was incapable of holding Him all in
I fell to the floor

I had finally experienced Him

"And this, so that I may know Him [experientially, becoming more thoroughly acquainted with Him, understanding the remarkable wonders of His Person more completely] and [in that same way experience] the power of His resurrection [which overflows and is active in believers]." Philippians 3:10a, AMP

Time Management

I struggled with managing my time

Juggling responsibilities

Fighting procrastination

So much on my plate

So little time to do it all

It's quite impressive how

He only needed six days

To create the universe

Six days to create what takes eternity to explore

Not seven. Six days

Because Abba still made time to rest

Might not be a bad idea

To ask Him His strategy for time management

"Commit your works to the Lord [submit and trust them to Him], and your plans will succeed [if you respond to His will and guidance]." Proverbs 16:3, AMP

Delay

I prayed against delay
It didn't make sense that
Others were accomplishing goals similar to mine
Yet I hadn't received a breakthrough

So, He asked me:
"If you didn't set the time, how do you know you are delayed?"

If Sarah and Abraham lived in our generation
People would have invited them to revivals on fruitfulness
The Bible says "Abraham believed God
and it was counted unto him as righteousness"

Do you know God's promises to you?
Or are you comparing your timeline to others
And praying against something that may not even apply to you?

"Yet God has made everything beautiful for its own time. He has planted eternity in the human heart, but even so, people cannot see the whole scope of God's work from beginning to end." Ecclesiastes 3:11, NLT

Attention to Detail

I got tired a lot
I thought it was low-iron
Until I almost passed out
Then He told me in a dream
That I needed to rest and make better diet choices

"You're not eating well," He said
"You won't last if you don't rest."
"Of what use is a dead lion?"

But how could He say that?
His last reference to a rest day for Himself
Was the seventh day of creation, forever ago
Yet, He talks about my rest
I told Him to go and rest first
And He chuckled

I had never heard Him laugh before
Do you know what would happen if he took a rest day? LOL!
However, I did become more intentional about my health and wellness

"He lay down and slept under the juniper tree, and behold, an angel touched him and said to him, 'Get up and eat.' He looked, and by his head there was a bread cake baked on hot coal, and a pitcher of water. So he ate and drank and lay down again. Then the angel of the Lord came again a second time and touched him and said, 'Get up, and eat, for the journey is too long for you [without adequate sustenance].'" 1 Kings 19:5–7, AMP

A Respected King

He commands so much respect
I didn't quite understand how much
Until in a dream, I heard the angels talk about how privileged man is
To possess the free will to choose
while still operating under His gift of grace and redemption

With angels, His word is law
With instructions executed exactly as ordered
When the angel Lucifer attempted treason
He was cast away, with his supporting crew
Destined to be punished forever

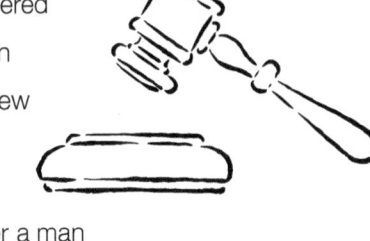

In 1 Kings 13, a lion was sent to slaughter a man
It slaughtered the man and stood next to a donkey
It didn't touch the donkey or any of the people walking by
Because the instruction was for the lion to kill only the man

In Daniel 10, an angel was sent with the answer to Daniel's prayers
Although this angel was intercepted by the prince of Persia
He waited until another angel, Michael, came to help him
Because God forbid that the first angel should return to heaven
Without fulfilling the mission on which he was sent

Do you understand the kind of authority He commands?

"Who is there who speaks and it comes to pass, unless the Lord
has authorized and commanded it?" Lamentations 3:37, AMP

Hungry Demons

The day He stops loving me is the day I die

After praying, fasting, breaking strongholds

Waging war against the enemy's camp

Defeated demons waiting, salivating

Plotting their revenge

Hoping for the day He chooses to look away

That day will never come

Because His love never stops, His eyes never close

Absolutely nothing can separate me from the love of God

"Because you have made the Lord, [who is] my refuge, even the Most High, your dwelling place, no evil will befall you, nor will any plague come near your tent. For He will command His angels in regard to you, to protect and defend and guard you in all your ways [of obedience and service]. They will lift you up in their hands, so that you do not [even] strike your foot against a stone. You will tread upon the lion and cobra; the young lion and the serpent you will trample underfoot." Psalm 91:9–13, AMP

Your Temple

I screamed as loudly as I could
As he entered in and out of me
You said my body is Your temple
You were silent in the echo of my screams
You let him take a piece of me
Forcefully violating "Your temple"

The hours I would have spent singing melodies to You
I spent scrubbing myself in the shower
Attempting to wash his pigged-self off my soul
The sleep I would have welcomed as hours of restful escape
I used to relive the experience through vivid dreams

Don't You owe me an explanation?
I've bleached the purity stains of my blanket
Can You bleach my soul?
I've healed from the stitched-up wounds
Can You take away the scars?

Worst of all, he left a seed
And it almost feels like You watered it
A life I'm forced to love
Yet You ask me to pray
Silence and tears are all I have left to give

"And at the ninth hour Jesus cried with a loud voice, saying,
'Eloi, Eloi, lama sabachthani?' – which is translated, 'My God,
my God, why have you forsaken me?'" Mark 15:34, AMP

Loss

Nothing prepares you for the loss of a loved one
Not how many books read
Or number of classes attended

As if that wasn't bad enough
You're assured by expert commentators that it is God's doing
"The Lord giveth and the Lord taketh away"
"They are in a better place"

If that were the case
Why are You just as broken as I am?
Why do You give comfort in loss?
Why do You send encouragement?

*"For the Lord will not reject forever, for if He causes grief, then He will
have compassion according to His abundant lovingkindness and tender
mercy. For He does not afflict willingly and from His heart or grieve the
children of men." Lamentations 3:31–33, AMP*

Sacrifice

He grew wings

If I caught a feather, I could keep it

I struggled with returning barbule feather strands in gratitude

Tithing ten percent of my earnings

Offering my desired gifts to God

He already had more

I wondered why He would request some of my little

He doesn't want or need any of it

He wants me

Sacrifice isn't giving up what hurts me

Sacrifice is giving up what comforts me, which hurts

One of the best ways to show love is to give

He gave His most invaluable gift, His son

Hoping that I would love Him enough to offer a gift as well

In addition to giving Him a portion of my treasures

If I don't add myself, my time, my will to the altar

Then is it truly a sacrifice?

Jesus' gift was His body, His blood, His life

It'll be an insult to think I can buy my way out of being the sacrifice

"For I desire and delight in [steadfast] loyalty [faithfulness in the covenant relationship], rather than sacrifice, and in the knowledge of God more than burnt offerings." Hosea 6:6, AMP

Entitlement

I often catch myself saying

"Thank you, Lord, for loving me, even when I don't deserve it"

As if there are moments I actually deserve His love

"For it is by grace [God's remarkable compassion and favor drawing you to Christ] that you have been saved [actually delivered from judgment and given eternal life] through faith. And this [salvation] is not of yourselves [not through your own effort], but it is the [undeserved, gracious] gift of God." Ephesians 2:8, AMP

Paintings

I have all these silly ideas, goals, and dreams
And I often come around to share them with Him
Instead, He lets us paint them together

When I ask His opinion on what we should paint, He always has an idea
He lets me pick my colors, tools, and methods
Spilling paint on myself
Messing up the walls of His presence
And getting some paint on Him

When we're done, He cleans me up
And gives me another paintbrush with a blank canvas
It brings Him joy to see me happy, making an effort
And using resources He has provided

Regardless of how much I may "mess up" my piece
He provides another fresh brush and canvas
To encourage me to keep working

"But Jesus called them to Himself, saying [to the apostles], 'Allow the children to come to Me, and do not forbid them, for the kingdom of God belongs to such as these.'" Luke 18:16, AMP

Focus

It only took a few breaths
Before the same lips who praised me
Tore me to shreds

In life, everyone is given a full glass of water to hold
And a slender bar to walk on
Those who hail praises are on the left
And those who criticize, on the right

When I make a mistake, a tumble, a possible debacle
The critics take the throne
Shredding and shaming, online and offline
While I'll feel distraught
I'll need to take heed, lest I fall

When I pull off a stunt without a spill
Stacks of praises are bestowed
While I'm thrilled about the attention and accolades
The thin line that borders excitement and distraction becomes blurry
I still must take heed, lest I fall

Those successful are not distracted by accolades or criticism
They are focused on protecting the contents of their glass
And making it past the bar

There are only six days

Between Palm Sunday and the Crucifixion

Six days

Before the same mouths who praised Jesus, killed Him

Six days for a celebrated hero

To be judged a criminal and crucified

If you're basking in the accolades

Or assimilating derogatory statements from critics

You might be heading for a fall

Don't let the excitement get to your head

Don't let the critics get to your heart

Pick up your glass

Fill yourself up with kind words

And get back on your bar

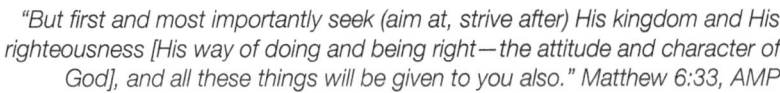

"But first and most importantly seek (aim at, strive after) His kingdom and His righteousness [His way of doing and being right—the attitude and character of God], and all these things will be given to you also." Matthew 6:33, AMP

Bars

I set them for myself

And then I smashed them on the first trial

People asked, "What's next?"

So, I set another goal and smashed it again

This new accomplishment built me a platform of supporters

Still, everyone keeps asking, "What's next?"

Recognition after recognition

I come home to the same pillows

The same thoughts

The same me

People see me differently

I see myself as the same

I realized I needed something that transcended statistics and accolades

I told God I wanted a life worthy to become a timeless memory

Lived in accordance with His will and purpose for me

Knowing and loving Him forever

"So I became great and excelled more than all who preceded me in Jerusalem. My wisdom also remained with me. Whatever my eyes looked at with desire I did not refuse them. I did not withhold from my heart any pleasure, for my heart was pleased because of all my labor; and this was my reward for all my labor. Then I considered all which my hands had done and labored to do, and behold, all was vanity and chasing after the wind and there was no profit (nothing of lasting value) under the sun." Ecclesiastes 2:9–11, AMP

Listen

When I'm sought out for encouragement
I cringe in fear of saying something wrong

So, He taught me how to listen
Because there is truly no wrong way to listen

"Understand this, my beloved brothers and sisters. Let everyone be quick to hear [be a careful, thoughtful listener], slow to speak [a speaker of carefully chosen words and], slow to anger [patient, reflective, forgiving]." James 1:19, AMP

Target

The thief comes to steal, kill, and destroy

If you don't have anything worth stealing, killing, or destroying

The thief has no business with you

If you're considered a target

Understand that you're extremely valuable

"When the devil had finished every temptation, he [temporarily]
left Him until a more opportune time." Luke 4:13, AMP

Pillars

The best of friends

Are usually not the ones that wait

Until the final product hits the global market

To say, *"your work is good"*

But those who choose to be used as your canvas

Who go back and forth with you

Editing business proposals

Exploring expansion strategies

Taking the messes, spills, and stray bullets

Splotches, drips, and smears

While encouraging you to keep trying

Until you hit success

"But Moses' hands were heavy and he grew tired. So, they took a stone and put it under him, and he sat on it. Then Aaron and Hur held up his hands, one on one side and one on the other side; so it was that his hands were steady until the sun set. So Joshua overwhelmed and defeated Amalek and his people with the edge of the sword." Exodus 17:12–13, AMP

Love Languages

What is Your love language?
You love all your children
But there are a few
Who make You feel like the only God
Who depend on you like You're their only help
Who praise You like it's the first time

Since You bask in the praises of Your people
I picked "words of affirmation"
But is that really Your love language?

I think on the number of times You've modeled generosity
And advised not to come into Your presence empty-handed
So maybe "receiving gifts"
But is that really Your love language?

Then You say "those who love Me will spend time with Me"
So, I settled on "quality time"
Because a relationship with You supersedes accomplishing deeds for You
But is that really Your love language?

So I asked the Holy Spirit, "what is your love language?"
And He responded, "Obedience"

"If you [really] love Me, you will keep and obey
My commandments." John 14:15, AMP

The God Factor

If I can give you a solid explanation
Step by step
On how I got to where I currently am
Then do I truly have God?

If I can show you calculations and plans
Day by day
Of how my accomplishments in life fell into place
Then do I truly have God?

When you ride with Him
There has to be someplace, somewhere, sometime
That cannot be explained

Like how King Xerxes couldn't sleep
Because God wanted to bless Mordecai
Mordecai woke up to honor and celebration
He would never be able
to explain why, all of a sudden, His Majesty couldn't sleep

The "God factor"

*"The king's heart is like channels of water in the hand of the Lord;
He turns it whichever way He wishes." Proverbs 21:1, AMP*

Victory

I am certain of victory
Because the One who goes before me
Is undefeated

I make strides in grace
Because the One who sails my ship
Commands the wind

I am guaranteed a win
Because my Hero
Is the One leading the war

I confess His words on my lips
And have allowed it to become my conviction
My doubts don't limit His capacity
My frail efforts don't restrict Him

He is God all by Himself
First and only of His kind
Forever undefeated

"What then shall we say to all these things? If God is for us, who can be [successful] against us?" Romans 8:31, AMP

A Fly on the Wall

While I prided myself in confidence and competence
He saw through my oblivious heart
Listened to conversations I couldn't hear
Attended meetings I wasn't invited to
Observed the hearts of some towards me
And carefully sifted the wheat from the chaff

I would wake up with supernatural guidance
A form of direction, an instruction
Or perhaps a stern warning

So, I prayed for the gift of discernment
And to remain obedient to His leading

"Now when they had gone, an angel of the Lord appeared to Joseph in a dream and said, 'Get up! Take the Child and His mother and flee to Egypt, and remain there until I tell you; for Herod intends to search for the Child in order to destroy Him.' So, Joseph got up and took the Child and His mother while it was still night, and left for Egypt." Matthew 2:13–14, AMP

Rapture

Living abroad won't satisfy you

Running away won't protect you

Foreign currency won't save you

Multiple colored passports won't preserve you

The only guarantee to eternal life is submission to Jesus

Being intentional about living righteously, in obedience

You'll need His help

I'll need His help

To be saved from the impending doom of torment in Hell

Or torture for those left behind who refuse the mark of the beast

Even the church might be a part of the mix

Secure your salvation now

Ask Him for guidance

"'Behold, I (Jesus) am coming quickly, and My reward is with Me, to give to each one according to the merit of his deeds (earthly works, faithfulness). I am the Alpha and the Omega, the First and the Last, the Beginning and the End [the Eternal One].' Blessed (happy, prosperous, to be admired) are those who wash their robes [in the blood of Christ by believing and trusting in Him—the righteous who do His commandments], so that they may have the right to the tree of life, and may enter by the gates into the city. Outside are the dogs [the godless, the impure, those of low moral character] and the sorcerers [with their intoxicating drugs, and magic arts], and the immoral persons [the perverted, the molesters, and the adulterers], and the murderers, and the idolaters, and everyone who loves and practices lying (deception, cheating)." Revelation 22:12–15, AMP

When Stars Align

I had promised myself that I wouldn't fall for anything
Until He came for my heart, and my walls came shattering

When He comes for you, you'll fall hard
But if you push Him away, outside your life
Then He'll become the One outside, knocking

Not because He can't leave
Not because there aren't others in need of His attention
But because He isn't ready to give up on you

His heart believes
That one day, when stars align
You'll want to come outside
And take a walk with Him

*"Behold, I stand at the door [of the church] and continually knock.
If anyone hears My voice and opens the door, I will come in and eat
with him (restore him), and he with Me." Revelation 3:20, AMP*

Deployed

"Excuse me, that's where I sit every Sunday"
Marking territories in a house built for the broken
You don't move into a hospital room after being discharged
You leave to keep up with healthy activities of your daily living
You honor scheduled clinic visits for periodic checkups
In order to prevent another full-blown admission

In the same light, you attend frequent saint gatherings
to get electrified and encouraged
You study God's Word and draw others to Him
In speech, conduct, and mannerisms
When you're empowered, you share your testimony
You allow room for others seeking redemption
Pulling them to your Source that never runs dry

Your claim to be a Christian shouldn't only be seen on Sundays
When you wrestle with the broken
over a hospital bed you've been discharged from
Your claim to be a Christian should be seen
Where policies are being created in government
Where decrees are being made in the palaces of kings and queens
Where laws are being executed in the marketplace
Christians ought to be empowered to seek purposeful territorial influence
in their assignments, then deployed to the marketplace as salt and light

*"And He said to them, 'Go into all the world and preach
the gospel to all creation.'" Mark 16:15, AMP*

Power

The force behind motion

Also called gas, petrol, fuel, diesel

Works to induce energy and facilitate movement

He has several names

While some take advantage of His power

And make accomplishments in their purpose

Some choose to sit and argue

About which church type is superior

Whether church X has more access to God than church W

Like asking whether gas moves faster than petrol

Mindless argument

A select few believe He doesn't exist at all

Running on empty

The Bible says Jesus is the way

"All authority in heaven and on earth has been given to Me"

If a body of worship doesn't acknowledge Jesus

Or teach you more about Him

Find and attend one that does

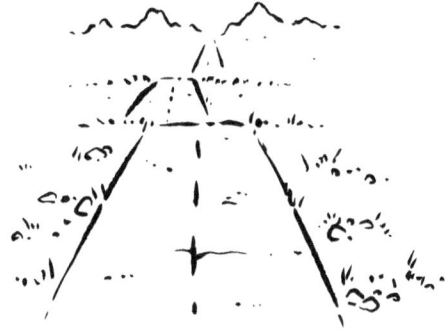

"The [spiritually ignorant] fool has said in his heart,
'There is no God.'" Psalm 14:1a, AMP

Humans

If you live for their acclamation

You'll die from their silence

"Don't put your confidence in powerful people; there is no help for you there. When they breathe their last, they return to the earth, and all their plans die with them. But joyful are those who have the God of Israel as their helper, whose hope is in the Lord their God." Psalm 146:3–5, NLT

Sin

Sometimes sin appears good-looking
Giving wings to my critical judgment

Sometimes sin provides a warm embrace
Comforting as fire in cold winter

Sometimes sin pays with currency
Purchasing me some respect in decision-making rooms

Sometimes sin promotes my satiety
Sexual urges in and out of self-gratification

Only no one told me
Its good looks are a glossy paint coating, masking rusted metal
Its promises are ephemeral
Its comfort is withering

The more I breathe it in
The more tarnished my lungs become
Multiple steps closer to destruction
But I'm too oblivious to see
That time with it will cost me much more
than I expected to pay

*"For the wages of sin is death, but the free gift of God [that is,
His remarkable, overwhelming gift of grace to believers] is
eternal life in Christ Jesus our Lord." Romans 6:23, AMP*

Love

I used to doubt the existence of true love
I thought it was a stroke of luck
Until He reminded me that He is love
So, if I thought love was nonexistent
Then that means I thought He was inexistent

I tried to explain my doubts about love
Then, He took me to 1 Corinthians 13
Asked me to replace Love with God, and re-read

God is patient
God is kind
God does not envy
God does not boast
God is not proud
God does not dishonor others

God is not self-seeking

God is not easily angered

God keeps no record of wrongs

God does not delight in evil

God rejoices with the truth

God always protects

God always trusts

God always hopes

God always perseveres

God never fails

Since we are to be like Christ

He asked me to replace His name with mine and make it my confession

If there was an attribute that didn't quite fit

It was my assignment to work on it

In order for me to become like Christ

Assignment: *Make 1 Corinthians 13:4–8 your daily confession*

Detachment

God gifted Isaac to Abraham
And later requested for his life

Abraham did not end up sacrificing Isaac
But Isaac had died in the heart of Abraham
Before they embarked on their journey to Mount Moriah

The ability to detach from the gift
And remain in love with the Giver
Is a skill every Christian would need to master

"Looking at him, Jesus felt a love (high regard, compassion) for him, and He said to him, "You lack one thing: go and sell all your property and give [the money] to the poor, and you will have [abundant] treasure in heaven; and come, follow Me [becoming My disciple, believing and trusting in Me and walking the same path of life that I walk]." But the man was saddened at Jesus' words, and he left grieving, because he owned much property and had many possessions [which he treasured more than his relationship with God]." Mark 10:21–22, AMP

Value

Preparation happens when you're hidden, so don't rush the process

Learn and master your skill

When Pharaoh sent for Joseph from prison

There was only enough time to shave and change clothes

before responding to the call

That wasn't the time to learn or develop dream interpretation skills

or whatever Joseph hadn't mastered before the call

Joseph interpreted Pharaoh's dream and provided a worthy solution

Although Pharaoh hadn't asked for a solution yet, Joseph offered one

So, Pharaoh allowed him the opportunity to become the solution

Because honor will always be given to value providers

So, stay ready to offer value

Opportunity may knock when you least expect

Perhaps Joseph would have gone back to prison for life

if he hadn't provided value

Be resourceful! Provide great and practical solutions

Don't sleep on your skill

"But at midnight there was a shout, 'Look! The bridegroom [is coming]! Go out to meet him.' Then all those virgins got up and put their own lamps in order [trimmed the wicks and added oil and lit them]. But the foolish virgins said to the wise, 'Give us some of your oil, because our lamps are going out.' But the wise replied, 'No, otherwise there will not be enough for us and for you, too; go instead to the dealers and buy oil for yourselves.' But while they were going away to buy oil, the bridegroom came, and those who were ready went in with him to the wedding feast; and the door was shut and locked." Matthew 25:6–10, AMP

All-Knowing

I know I've met Him
Because I have changed
I'm no longer waiting for people to meet my standards
I've changed myself to meet His standards

I know I've met Him
Because I've changed
I no longer pay attention to preconceived notions people have
About my past and future sins

We're like two people sitting through a movie
One who already saw it (Him)
And I, watching it for the first time
This movie happens to be my life

While I'm nervous about what the next scene brings
– *anxious about tomorrow*
He isn't nervous, because He has already seen it
Because He knows the end from the beginning
So, I've learned to trust Him
And wait expectantly for the next scene

"It is the Lord who goes before you; He will be with you. He will not fail you or abandon you. Do not fear or be dismayed." Deuteronomy 31:8, AMP

Grief

Sometimes it's not about saying the right words
Or telling someone *"I know how you feel"*
As if I actually do
Or maybe I am too scared
To express my ignorance of the feeling

And even if I did in fact know
Grief is like a rainbow
A mix of colors put together
Like the mix of emotions endured
Sadness, depression, tears, anger, denial
No matter how well it is explained
I'll never truly be able to touch it, feel it, or truly understand

What's worse are the unseen highways that connect the colors
How one can be laughing now and crying the next second
I'll never know what color spectrum the person grieving will be
So, I'll stay present, accepting and available
Waiting patiently on them
As Jesus would have done for me

"Rejoice with those who rejoice [sharing others' joy], and weep with those who weep [sharing others' grief]." Romans 12:15, AMP

Expectations

People wiped Jesus' tears and wailed with Him while He carried His cross

A lot were hurt by Jesus' pain

But the Bible didn't record anyone offering to help Him carry the cross

and Simon of Cyrene was compelled to do so

If helping Jesus carry the cross was going to come in the way of His destiny

Jesus would have rebuked him, just like He did Peter in Matthew 16

Prior to carrying the cross

Jesus was whipped with a flagellum, a lead-tipped whip

Designed to quickly remove flesh from the body of its victim

Imagine carrying a wooden cross over those freshly opened wounds

Jesus impacted the lives of millions of people

Yet no one offered to help when He was suffering

Including His disciples

If you're expecting the people you've helped to return the favor

You're orchestrating a high-end disappointment

Do what you can, if you can, with what you can afford

Following the bloody footprints of the One who came before

Not expecting a repayment

"But love [that is, unselfishly seek the best or higher good for] your enemies, and do good, and lend, expecting nothing in return; for your reward will be great (rich, abundant), and you will be sons of the Most High; because He Himself is kind and gracious and good to the ungrateful and the wicked. Be merciful (responsive, compassionate, tender) just as your [heavenly] Father is merciful." Luke 6:35–36, AMP

Pointing Fingers

You and I have the power to stop things

However, there are some things I've let slide

That I shouldn't have

And then there are more obvious things

That we've let slide

Like how we stay subscribed to streaming services

That have used their platform to reduce Jesus to a commoner

They may not have created those visual productions

But they lifted it to fame

Which encouraged the mockery of a hero

Their crime is no different from mine, it's just more obvious

God isn't going to judge me any differently

So, I'll still focus on my journey

While I speak up

And show my stance on global issues

I'm careful to watch

the little ways I've mocked Him

It only looks like I haven't

Because everyone's magnifying glasses

Are focused on another with more clout

"Why do you look at the [insignificant] speck that is in your brother's eye, but do not notice and acknowledge the [egregious] log that is in your own eye?" Matthew 7:3, AMP

Risk

One of the greatest threats to *our faithfulness to God*

Is success

Success breeds complacency

Every time God exalts us, He is taking a risk

A risk of more time being spent with the gift

And less time with the Giver

A risk of us conveniently leaving out His name

When we're asked how we have become so accomplished

A risk of us believing that *"If I did it before, I can do it again"*

And forgetting that it's the hand of God that makes the difference

Precious gifts are mostly given to people who can be trusted

Can God trust you?

Are you going to remain faithful to Him after he enriches you?

"The king said thoughtfully, 'Is not this the great Babylon which I myself have built as the royal residence and seat of government by the might of my power and for the honor and glory of my majesty?' While the words were still in the king's mouth, a voice came [as if falling] from heaven, saying, 'O King Nebuchadnezzar, to you it is declared: "The kingdom has been removed from you, and you will be driven away from mankind, and your dwelling place will be with the animals of the field. You will be given grass to eat like the cattle, and seven periods of time will pass over you until you know [without any doubt] that the Most High God rules over the kingdom of mankind and He bestows it on whomever He desires."' Daniel 4:30–32, AMP

Seed

He said, *"Ask anything in My name and I'll do it"*
So, I asked for a life lived like that of a palm tree
I asked for accomplishments that withstood the test of time
Never to be broken down by the credits, accolades, or critiques
Weathering through time and storms
Always overcoming successfully

He gave me a seed
I put the seed in the soil
Judiciously caring for it

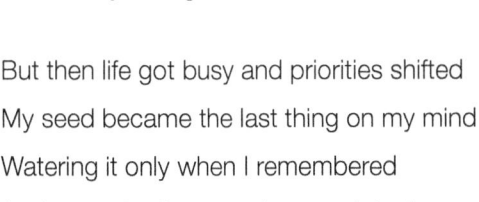

But then life got busy and priorities shifted
My seed became the last thing on my mind
Watering it only when I remembered
And giving it whatever else was left of me

Soon after, it hadn't grown into the vision I had
My work wasn't getting the credits I hoped for
My accomplishments weren't opening the doors I had prayed for
I asked God why He hadn't fulfilled His promise

And He asked me, *"was it the fault of the seed or a fault of yours?"*

"He who plants and he who waters are one [in importance and esteem,
working toward the same purpose]; but each will receive his own reward
according to his own labor." 1 Corinthians 3:8, AMP

The Lord Said

"The Lord said", a phrase largely used by His children
Who listen to His voice
And follow His instruction

It is also a phrase abused by cowards
To shut out the opinions of truth seekers
Because who are you to question my decision?
After I tell you, *"It's the Lord who said it"*

But, did the Lord really say it?
Or am I just too scared to admit that I don't know what I'm doing
That what you say might expose the flaws in my plan
Since I would rather have you not question me
I'll conceal my fears behind *"The Lord said…"*

I understand the place of faith
I respect those who actually hear Him and follow through

For those who have neither faith nor listening ears
Oftentimes, fear drives the ship
When they say, *"The Lord said…"*

"You shall not take the name of the Lord your God in vain [that is, irreverently, in false affirmations or in ways that impugn the character of God]; for the Lord will not hold guiltless nor leave unpunished the one who takes His name in vain [disregarding its reverence and its power]." Exodus 20:7, AMP

58

Fire

Trying to burn for God
While I date a fire extinguisher

"Do not be unequally bound together with unbelievers [do not make mismatched alliances with them, inconsistent with your faith]. For what partnership can righteousness have with lawlessness? Or what fellowship can light have with darkness?" 2 Corinthians 6:14, AMP

Leveled Field

God, the solution
Seems to have now become the problem

What started as communion
Man and God
Has evolved into an obligation

The book that was to serve as a guide
The Bible
Now misinterpreted out of context

The veil that was torn to equalize access to God's presence
Is being sewn back by leaders on high pedestals
Such that we think they could touch His feet
But somehow His other children can't?

I'll only know Him, as much as I've seen of Him
The only version of Him I'll confidently express
Is the version of Him that I've experienced

Blind Bartimaeus knew Him as the Healer
The guests at the wedding in Cana knew him as the Provider
The disciples during the storm knew Him as the Deliverer
The woman at the well knew him as the All-knowing One

Seeing that He has so many sides

What do I do with my gift of access to Him?

Do I spend the time getting to know more of Him?

Or do I hope that someone else does

So I can feed off their knowledge of Him?

As if I didn't have access to Him myself

Almost like begging for water to quench my thirst

From someone else's bucket

While He had already given a fresh stream of living water

For everyone to drink to their full

There is nothing wrong with seeking assistance from religious leaders

Especially in times when I feel too weak to stand

But if my Christianity is solely dependent on my leader

And if my walk with God suffers when my mortal shepherd falls into sin

Then I ought to check myself

My loyalty to God shouldn't be dependent on another human

Although access to God is now available to all

Access to His secret place of intimacy

Lies only on the bed of sacrifice

Am I willing to put in the work?

"For it is through Him that we both have a [direct] way of approach in one Spirit to the Father. So then you are no longer strangers and aliens [outsiders without rights of citizenship], but you are fellow citizens with the saints (God's people), and are [members] of God's household." Ephesians 2:18–19, AMP

Memories

Romantically, I've loved twice
But only truly been loved once
By my late husband

How do you describe someone
Who starts out as the standard and forever remains the one?
My babe was imperfect, but truly an angel

Although I lavished you with countless expressions
of how much I loved you
Love wasn't enough to keep you here with me
I've been blessed by you
I've become a better person because of you
I understand the intricacies of love, only after being loved by you

I pray the angels give you wings to fly
Because selfless souls like yours
Deserve all the happiness there is to offer

I hope my castle is next to yours
In case God gives us a chance
To choose one another in the afterlife
Until then, rest in power

Dedicated to loving spouses now lost
Persons who stayed ever-present
Forever remaining our most cherished blessings

Fruitful Money

Judas, the second person I had questions for, after Eve

Questions on how he could betray his friend, his brother, for money

Thirty pieces of silver has an estimated worth of USD 90-450, as of 2020

Perhaps more valuable at the time since it was enough to purchase a field

Humanity was let down for the fruit of a tree

A craving of Eve that led to being exiled

Out of the garden of innocence and enjoyment

Jesus was betrayed for money

Money that was later dumped

after Judas experienced the guilt that led to his suicide

While I parade myself in my judgment hat

I'm reminded that I've let God down for less

Sometimes even without reason or reward

Who am I to judge?

"Do not judge and criticize and condemn [others unfairly with an attitude of self-righteous superiority as though assuming the office of a judge], so that you will not be judged [unfairly]. For just as you[hypocritically] judge others [when you are sinful and unrepentant], so will you be judged; and in accordance with your standard of measure [used to pass out judgment], judgment will be measured to you." Matthew 7:1–2, AMP

Turns

Jesus' temptations were not the devil's first attempt

to sway someone off purpose

Your temptations will not be his last

The smell of success attracts attention

The good and the bad

Satan took Jesus to a very high mountain

Showed Him the kingdoms of the world in their splendor

And offered it to Jesus in exchange for His submission

Jesus stood His ground

He understood His purpose

And knew this was bait

An attempt to distract and terminate His mission

If you smell of success and are faithful in your consecration

A time will come when it'll be you at that pinnacle

Listening to words capable of swaying you

Hoping you'll exchange your purpose and zeal for material gain

What would you say?

"For what does it benefit a man to gain the whole world [with all its pleasures], and forfeit his soul?" Mark 8:36, AMP

First Step

The first discipline is to start

Start that book, register that business

The naysayers seem to be loudest in the beginning

Because your supporters' club hasn't developed enough

to propose an opposing argument on your behalf

Every beginner possesses a higher propensity to fail

Falling off a bike, learning to walk

Isn't it better to fail early, while you master your skill?

The glory you seek will happen only if you're courageous enough to start

And then to continue after the first step

If Jesus hadn't started His work

He would probably have been called *"the carpenter's son"* all His life

Even Jesus had to work to prove Himself as *"the Messiah"*

He spent time away from home, slept in random places

So He could fulfill His mission of spreading the gospel

Whatever has been given to you is good enough to start

The journey might be unpredictable and uncomfortable

But be encouraged to take that first step

"Whatever your hand finds to do, do it with all your might; for there is no activity or planning or knowledge or wisdom in Sheol (the nether world, the place of the dead) where you are going." Ecclesiastes 9:10, AMP

Privilege

"Master, carest Thou not that we perish?" Mark 4:38
Although the same storm that hit the disciples also hit Jesus
They all looked to Him to deliver them
The disciples knew that even though everyone on the boat was human
There was something different about Jesus' kind of human,
perhaps a super-human
The storm would have to react to Jesus differently
Because He was privileged with supernatural power

In order for the disciples to make it out alive
They needed the covering of Jesus
So they cried, "Master, carest Thou not that we perish?"
And Jesus saved them with the power that came
with the privilege of His position

In less exotic ways
We have all been given some level of privilege
Spiritual, racial, gender, ethnic, wealth/class privileges
In what ways have we stood up for others with lesser privilege?

Jesus could have saved only Himself
But He chose to save the others who couldn't help themselves
While empowering them with the knowledge
that faith is needed to conquer storms
Again, *in what ways have you empowered those with lesser privilege?*

> *"But a Samaritan (foreigner), who was traveling, came upon him; and when he saw him, he was deeply moved with compassion [for him], and went to him and bandaged up his wounds, pouring oil and wine on them [to sooth and disinfect the injuries]; and he put him on his own pack-animal, and brought him to an inn and took care of him." Luke 10:33-34, AMP*

A Returned Package

The father denied it
The father didn't know
The father wasn't ready

The mother wasn't ready
The mother didn't want this seed

While families lay at His feet seeking and praying
"Father, give me a child"

A soul returned to God
"It didn't seem like I was needed by the ones I was sent to"

"Before I formed you in the womb I knew you [and approved of you as My chosen instrument], and before you were born I consecrated you [to Myself as My own]; I have appointed you as a prophet to the nations." Jeremiah 1:5, AMP

The *"Hood"*

Pregnant-hood

Loss of teeth, hair, sense of smell, and memory

Back and pelvic pain

Loss of appetite but with weight gain

Gestational diabetes

Pre-eclampsia

Anemia

Acne

Yeast infections

Edema

Blood spotting

Urine leaks and incontinence

Nausea and vomiting

Indigestion

Stretch marks and cellulite

Vaginal tears, unhealing wounds, and permanent scars

Carpal tunnel

Postpartum depression

For a select few, grace has made pregnancy a walk in the park

Some experience some symptoms; some experience all

Imagine going through that and then losing the baby during delivery

Body shaming, pressure to "snap back"

Insensitive in-laws

Pressure to have physical intimacy during the healing process

Yet a number of us forget

To wish mothers a happy Mother's Day

A few men complain about the dwindling lights

in the attractiveness of their female partners

Some sit in decision-making rooms

And dictate pregnancy laws

Debates on how birth control is a woman's responsibility

And not a vasectomy

Pregnancy really could be seen as a shadow of death

A celebration party should be thrown

For everyone who survives the experience

"Even though I walk through the [sunless] valley of the shadow of death,
I fear no evil, for You are with me; Your rod [to protect] and Your staff
[to guide], they comfort and console me." Psalm 23:4, AMP

Manhood

The double standards

The unnecessary scrutiny

Lessons on how to suppress emotions

Before emotions were learned

Too close to children – pedophile?

Disagree with a woman – mansplaining?

Acting on sexual urges at the wrong time – rapist?

Lusting after someone a little too long – pervert?

Always defending men – misogynist?

Feeling sad, depressed, emotional – unmanly?

Nice or nerdy – boring?

Too ambitious – workaholic?

Too stylish – gay?

Overly confident – narcissist?

Not to say that anyone accused of any of these is guilty or innocent

But it is crazy, the egg-shells gentlemen have to walk on

Just so they're not mislabeled

"Blessed [morally courageous and spiritually alive with life-joy in God's goodness] are you when people insult you and persecute you, and falsely say all kinds of evil things against you because of [your association with] Me. Be glad and exceedingly joyful, for your reward in heaven is great [absolutely inexhaustible]." Matthew 5:11–12a, AMP

Adulthood

A scam.

LOL.

Singlehood

A time celebrated to wine and dine

Youth at its peak

Forgetting that it'll be the most time I'll ever have

As an independent adult

With the least amount of responsibilities

Still, I cannot seem to make time for Him

"Remember [thoughtfully] also your Creator in the days of your youth [for you are not your own, but His], before the evil days come or the years draw near when you will say [of physical pleasures], "I have no enjoyment and delight in them." Ecclesiastes 12:1, AMP

Womanhood

A gem lost on the soils of the corporate Americas

A gem underappreciated on the soils of Africa

A gem under-voiced on the soils of the Middle East

A gem regardless

Still fighting for equality

Not particularly voiceless

Just deliberately silenced

Or preferably unheard

"The [very] stone which the builders rejected and threw away, has become the chief Cornerstone; This is the Lord's doing, and it is marvelous and wonderful in our eyes.'" Matthew 21:42b, AMP

Parenthood

Endless nerves and worries

Am I going to be a good parent?

Are they going to end up successful?

Am I going to provide everything needed?

Are they going to appreciate me for doing the best I could?

Am I going to be open enough to discuss uncomfortable topics?

Are they going to shut me out?

Am I going to be too strict, too cool, too difficult, too easily fooled?

Are they going to love and be loved in return?

Am I going to subconsciously suffocate their dreams with my ambition?

Are they going to hate me for executing the rules of our household?

Am I going to be an overbearing parent?

Are they going to think I'm too spiritual for involving God in everything?

Am I going to embarrass them with lame jokes?

Are they going to make fun of me behind my back?

I pray they don't do drugs

I pray they make good friends

I pray for God's protection over them

I pray they don't die before they are old and gray

I pray I prepare them for the world of cruel and judgmental people

Can I actually do this?

Sometimes I feel like the verse about worries and riches

Was written specifically for parents

No matter what we do

We cannot add a naturally growing hair strand to the heads of our children

We can only try to set a good enough example

And wholeheartedly pray for them

Adding calluses to our knees

Like our livelihood depended on their survival

"And why are you worried about clothes? See how the lilies and wildflowers of the field grow; they do not labor nor do they spin [wool to make clothing], yet I say to you that not even Solomon in all his glory and splendor dressed himself like one of these. But if God so clothes the grass of the field, which is alive and green today and tomorrow is [cut and] thrown [as fuel] into the furnace, will He not much more clothe you? You of little faith!" Matthew 6:28–30, AMP

Motherhood

Just like my decision about what I'll have for dinner
shouldn't raise an upheaval
I should be able to choose which way to have my baby
and have peace in the streets

So what if someone had a miscarriage?
So what if someone used in-vitro fertilization (IVF) to have their baby?
So what if someone had a delivery without medication?
So what if someone needed all the medications available?
So what if someone would like a vaginal delivery?
So what if someone prefers a Cesarean section?
So what if someone chooses not to have any children?
So what if someone opts for a surrogate?
So what if someone adopts a child?

Why are people so judgmental about this topic?
Wasn't Joseph Jesus' surrogate father?

"An angel of the Lord appeared to him in a dream saying, 'Joseph, descendant of David, do not be afraid to take Mary as your wife, for the Child who has been conceived in her is of the Holy Spirit.'" Matthew 1:20b, AMP

End of the *"Hood"*

Test of Love

His Son died

The most embarrassing, shameful death

The kind of death reserved for criminals

The only other person who was put through a similar test was Abraham

His task was to offer Isaac, his son, as a sacrifice unto God

Because of Abraham's loyalty and obedience

God stopped him before the sacrifice

And provided a replacement

He allowed Abraham to keep Isaac

And blessed his generation for it

But His own Son, Jesus, died

Just like Abraham was loyal, Jesus was loyal

But unlike Isaac, there was no substitute worthy of taking Jesus' place

God watched Him bleed on His journey to the cross

Watched as the thorns pierced through His head

Watched as people spat on Him

Watched as nails went through His flesh

Watched Him scream out in pain as alcohol soaked His wounds

And turned His face away as Jesus hung on the cross

God couldn't bear to see Him in pain

Or to see the sins of the world on His shoulders

And Jesus wailed

The healer, the powerful, the confident Jesus, wailed on the cross

There is nothing worse than being abandoned

By your most supportive partner

In your most vulnerable moment

Perhaps the Trinity had discussed among themselves

The need for death for the restoration of humanity to God

They understood the pain, the suffering

Even an angel was sent to strengthen Jesus at Gethsemane

Did they discuss the abandonment?

If they did, why did Jesus feel so alone?

Why did He ask, *"Father, Father, why hast thou forsaken me?"*

Did the Father know that He would be so affected by Jesus' pain

That He wouldn't be able to watch the process?

Did He know that He would forsake Him?

And where was the Holy Spirit? *The Great Comforter*

God did nothing

He didn't send an animal like the one He provided to replace Isaac

He couldn't have a sinful person take His place

No one was worthy of replacing Jesus

Do you think the One who parted the seas couldn't have saved His Son?

The One who walked in a heated furnace with the Hebrew friends

The One who wiped out creation with a flood

And rained manna and quail from heaven to cure hunger

God laid down His Almighty power

He put it under subjection

To demonstrate the meaning of love

So that you and I can have unlimited access to Him

This is why Love is the greatest, not power, joy, or peace

It is never the will of the Father

To put any devoted one through such pain and then forsake them

Because it's usually not the pain that hurts the most

It's the abandonment during the pain

Even His word says,

"When you go through the fire, I will be with you." Isaiah 43:2

"I will never leave you nor forsake you." Hebrews 13:5

And He never goes against His word

Yet, in the case of Jesus, His own Son

He acted out of character (against His word)

Because He thought about you and me

Because He loves you and me

So, He watched Him die

Sucked up His hurt

Sucked up His pain

And watched Him die

Something could replace Isaac

So, He intercepted death

But for the love of humankind

He allowed His to perish so mine could live

The finished definition of love on the cross

"No one has greater love [nor stronger commitment] than to lay down his own life for his friends." John 15:13, AMP

Stress

There was nothing supernatural
About Jesus' body reaction in the garden of Gethsemane

He may have experienced *hematohidrosis*
A rare condition that occurs
mostly during extreme physical or emotional stress
Where the capillaries that feed the sweat glands rupture
Causing the glands to leak blood
It's no surprise that the only disciple who documented this
was Luke, a physician

Have you ever been so stressed that your capillaries gave out?
And your sweat dropped like blood?
Think again before you accuse God
of not understanding extreme challenges

While Jesus experienced this level of stress
His disciples were asleep
No one was able to keep watch and pray with Him through His agony
How many friends in your *"close circle"* can fast and pray with you
Especially when you're at your lowest?

"When He arrived at the place [called Gethsemane], He said to them, 'Pray continually that you may not fall into temptation.' And He withdrew from them about a stone's throw, and knelt down and prayed, saying, 'Father, if You are willing, remove this cup [of divine wrath] from Me; yet not My will, but [always] Yours be done.' Now an angel appeared to Him from heaven, strengthening Him. And being in agony [deeply distressed and anguished; almost to the point of death], He prayed more intently; and His sweat became like drops of blood, falling down on the ground. When He rose from prayer, He came to the disciples and found them sleeping from sorrow." Luke 22:40–45, AMP

Dominate

There is no glory in poverty

There is no honor in mediocrity

The twenty-four elders lay their crowns at His feet

They already have crowns

God has blessed everyone with the ability to conquer

So go and conquer your space

Succeed in your career, excel in your marriage, thrive in ministry

Be victorious in everything your hands find to do

Be a domineering force in your discipline

Achieve success and earn your crown

So that you too can lay your crown at His feet

When He returns

God is the King of Kings

Not the King of mediocrity

"The man who had received five bags of gold brought the other five. 'Master,' he said, 'You entrusted me with five bags of gold. See, I have gained five more.' His master replied, 'Well done, good and faithful servant! You have been faithful with a few things; I will put you in charge of many things. Come and share your master's happiness!' The man with two bags of gold also came. 'Master,' he said, 'You entrusted me with two bags of gold; see, I have gained two more.' His master replied, 'Well done, good and faithful servant! You have been faithful with a few things; I will put you in charge of many things. Come and share your master's happiness!' Then the man who had received one bag of gold came. 'Master,' he said, 'I knew that you are a hard man, harvesting where you have not sown and gathering where you have not scattered seed. So I was afraid and went out and hid your gold in the ground. See, here is what belongs to you.' His master replied, 'You wicked, lazy servant! So, you knew that I harvest where I have not sown and gather where I have not scattered seed? Well then, you should have put my money on deposit with the bankers, so that when I returned, I would have received it back with interest. So, take the bag of gold from him and give it to the one who has ten bags.'" Matthew 25:20–28, NIV

Experience

I often questioned if I would have survived the Old Testament era
Because the character of God
Was one of law, order, and punishment

What's most fascinating
Is His character adjustment between the Old and New Testaments
How "obey or be destroyed" became "here are a few options; you choose"

Until I understood the fastest route to compassion is an experience
Carriers of the Human Immunodeficiency Virus (HIV)
were once treated like outcasts
Until HIV victims became the children in our homes
There always seems to be an attitude switch
When the problem hits our personal space
When a their-problem suddenly becomes an our-problem

In the same light
It wasn't until Jesus walked my shoes
Felt pain like me, understood my plight, and redeemed me to the Father
That God's "law and order" became "grace and love"
Only after Jesus became a man

"For we do not have a High Priest who is unable to sympathize and understand our weaknesses and temptations, but One who has been tempted [knowing exactly how it feels to be human] in every respect as we are, yet without [committing any] sin." Hebrews 4:15, AMP

Revenge

He had to make me understand

That being able to abuse my abuser

Wasn't the right approach on my journey to healing

"Beloved, never avenge yourselves, but leave the way open for God's wrath [and His judicial righteousness]; for it is written [in Scripture], 'Vengeance is Mine, I will repay,' says the Lord." Romans 12:19, AMP

Purity

I respect those who honor virginity until marriage
I am an advocate for that to minimize distractions
However, those who lose theirs beforehand, intentionally or accidentally
Will not have lesser crowns in heaven if they've repented

The thought behind celibacy is good
However, if I'm celibate so I can be painted by people as pure
But my heart is drenched in sin
Then am I truly pure?

If I choose to be celibate for spiritual reasons
Because sexual relations could cloud my sense of judgment
And I attempt to stay away from other non-sexual sins
Perhaps I'm truly on my purity journey

The presence or absence of a hymen
Shouldn't be a yardstick to measure purity

*"If we say we have no sin [refusing to admit that we are sinners], we delude
ourselves and the truth is not in us. [His word does not live in our hearts.]
If we [freely] admit that we have sinned and confess our sins, He is faithful
and just [true to His own nature and promises], and will forgive our sins
and cleanse us continually from all unrighteousness [our wrongdoing,
everything not in conformity with His will and purpose]." 1 John 1:8–9, AMP*

Forgiveness

We were raided
And I was molested
In the presence of my partner

He has begged for forgiveness
Pleaded, cried, wailed
Done everything to make it right

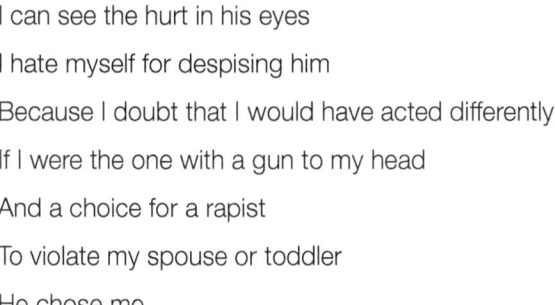

I can see the hurt in his eyes
I hate myself for despising him
Because I doubt that I would have acted differently
If I were the one with a gun to my head
And a choice for a rapist
To violate my spouse or toddler
He chose me

I'll need to forgive my partner, forgive the rapist, forgive other spectators
Forgive myself for developing PTSD and cringing at the sight of a man
Forgive myself for self-blaming and avoiding therapy
Forgive my dreams for re-living the experience
Forgive things I didn't know needed forgiving

Do you know how many forgiveness-*es* are required in any one act of sin?

"Then Peter came to him and asked, 'Lord, how many times will my brother sin against me and I forgive him and let it go? Up to seven times?' Jesus answered him, 'I say to you, not up to seven times, but seventy times seven.'" Matthew 18:21–22, AMP

The Great Provider

For every action in line with purpose
There is provision

Mary had only recently given birth to Jesus in Bethlehem
She probably hadn't unpacked her "birthing bag"
Neither Joseph nor Mary had any idea that in days
They would receive an urgent notice to leave their home
Because King Herod would be after Jesus' life

However, they experienced a visit from wise strangers
Men sent to honor Jesus
Who came bearing expensive gifts of gold, frankincense, and myrrh

After they left, an angel appeared to Joseph in a dream
And told him to leave town
"So he got up, took the child and his mother during the night and left."
This gives the impression that it all happened on the same night
or a few hours apart

Have you ever considered that there might not have been enough time
to pack a bag? Food, clothes, money?
But God, who is always thinking ahead, sent the wise strangers
To worship Jesus? Absolutely!
More importantly, to drop valuable gifts worth a lot

I'm not quite sure what Joseph packed for their urgent journey

I would first pack up the valuables

Gold, frankincense, and myrrh

Items that could easily be converted to money

Jesus spent the first three years of his life in Egypt

If Joseph didn't have enough money

Survival would have been challenging

But God sent valuables ahead

Whenever there is an instruction in line with purpose

Provision will always be made

Always

If you find yourself struggling with assignments, projects, or anything at all

Ask yourself, *"was I instructed to do this?"*

"And he said, 'This is what the Lord says: I will fill this valley with pools of water. For this is what the Lord says: You will see neither wind nor rain, yet this valley will be filled with water, and you, your cattle and your other animals will drink.'" 2 Kings 3:16–17, NIV

Ignorance

The audacity of people to think they can outrun Satan by themselves
he accrued experience as an angel and rose to a leadership position
he understands the powers and operation of angels
That's why he could stop an angel on a mission, in the Book of Daniel
And the archangel, Michael, had to intervene

After he was thrown out of heaven
he visited the Garden of Eden to deceive Adam and Eve
So, he has over 2000+ years of experience on earth
stealing, killing, and destroying

The temerity to think *"Although I got saved by God's grace
I can overcome the devil all by myself"*
How can you compete against someone
with over 2000 years of experience?
Do you really think you can outrun the schemes of the devil by yourself?
You're no match

Your power lies in the knowledge you have in the Word of God
and consistent prayer
Even though Jesus is the Word
Jesus still used the Word of God to overcome Satan
How much more you?

"Therefore, put on every piece of God's armor so you will be able to resist the enemy in the time of evil. Then after the battle you will still be standing firm. Stand your ground, putting on the belt of truth and the body armor of God's righteousness. For shoes, put on the peace that comes from the Good News so that you will be fully prepared. In addition to all of these, hold up the shield of faith to stop the fiery arrows of the devil. Put on salvation as your helmet, and take the sword of the Spirit, which is the word of God. Pray in the Spirit at all times and on every occasion. Stay alert and be persistent in your prayers for all believers everywhere." Ephesians 6:13–18, NLT

Gatekeeping

With all the information Jesus shared in the Bible

He didn't lose a precious stone from His crown reward

He is still seated on the right side of God

Every knee still bows at His name

Jesus has received His reward for His work

You also will receive a reward for your work

Showing others the way shouldn't result in your downfall

Sharing the knowledge you received shouldn't make you stumble

No candle ever went out by lighting other candles

There is no competition in the kingdom

There is space for everyone to shine

Information hoarding can only take you so far

If anything, it will limit how much you receive

Because you have become too selfish to give what was given to you

If God wants someone to know something

And you choose to gatekeep that knowledge

He'll use someone else to teach them

We are saved only because Jesus selflessly and graciously

showed us the way

"Heal the sick, raise the dead, cleanse the lepers, cast out demons. Freely you have received, freely give." Matthew 10:8, AMP

Born to War

The devil knows who I am, and I don't
The devil acknowledges the power of my will, and I don't
The devil recognizes the brightness of my star, and I don't

He tries for my confidence, tries for my time
Tries for my finances, my health, and my mind
Why is he so adamant about getting me?
Like God, what is it about man that the devil is also mindful of?

What a shame it is
For the devil to already know my strengths
To prioritize mastering the weaknesses of my ancestry
To leverage altars and covenants created in my bloodline
And carefully strategize attacks
While I dance with ignorance and sleep through prayer

For how long am I going to let him?
He has already lost to Jesus, so I know I'm built to conquer him
I only haven't because I'm unaware of the power I possess
in the blood of Jesus

*"For this reason also [because He obeyed and so completely humbled Himself],
God has highly exalted Him and bestowed on Him the name which is above every
name, so that at the name of Jesus every knee shall bow [in submission], of those
who are in heaven and on earth and under the earth, and that every tongue will
confess and openly acknowledge that Jesus Christ is Lord (sovereign God),
to the glory of God the Father." Philippians 2:9–11, AMP*

Doctrines

My goal is to know Him for myself

To study His patterns

To understand His ways

Not just in conformity to a preaching

Or as a paid respect to a minister

Or because it's my family's belief

With the countless amount of church doctrines we get slapped with

It's a steep slope trying not to get lost in church duties

In order not to forget that the goal is to know Him

People oppressing others with subconscious expectations

And for fear of not living up to it, "others" make commitments

To activities they cannot afford

To purposes that are not theirs

So that they don't fall short

Of someone else's expectation

As if that someone was the goal

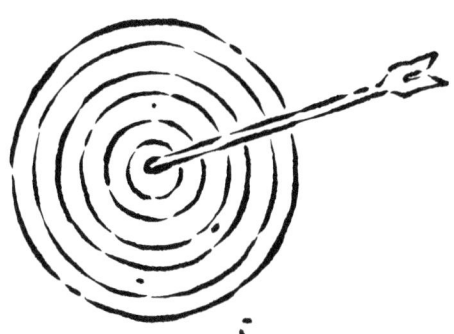

"Since we have gifts that differ according to the grace given to us, each of us is to use them accordingly: if [someone has the gift of] prophecy, [let him speak a new message from God to His people] in proportion to the faith possessed; if service, in the act of serving; or he who teaches, in the act of teaching," Romans 12:6–7, AMP

Growth

A state of transformation

From bringing treasures to be sacrificed at His altar

To becoming the treasure sacrificed at His altar

*"Therefore I urge you, brothers and sisters, by the mercies of God,
to present your bodies [dedicating all of yourselves, set apart]
as a living sacrifice, holy and well-pleasing to God, which is your
rational (logical, intelligent) act of worship." Romans 12:1, AMP*

Domestic Violence

he hit me again

The creator of my body has never hit me in anger

Yet this mortal loses his temper

And thinks hitting my body is how he'll find it

"Even so husbands should and are morally obligated to love their own wives as [being in a sense] their own bodies. He who loves his own wife loves himself. For no one ever hated his own body, but [instead] he nourishes and protects and cherishes it, just as Christ does the church, because we are members (parts) of His body. For this reason a man shall leave his father and his mother and shall be joined [and be faithfully devoted] to his wife, and the two shall become one flesh. This mystery [of two becoming one] is great; but I am speaking with reference to [the relationship of] Christ and the church. However, each man among you [without exception] is to love his wife as his very own self [with behavior worthy of respect and esteem, always seeking the best for her with an attitude of lovingkindness], and the wife [must see to it] that she respects and delights in her husband [that she notices him and prefers him and treats him with loving concern, treasuring him, honoring him, and holding him dear]." Ephesians 5:28-33, AMP

Love Motivations

Love is God vs. God is love
Symmetrical statements, yet context draws differences

"Love is God"
Here, the goal is to love
Motivated by passion
The freedom to love regardless of sex/gender
Because the goal is to love

"God is love"
The goal is God
Motivated by reverence for Him
Since He had said, man and wife
Rendering respect to His instruction
Man to woman, woman to man
Since the goal is God
Pleasing Him is the ultimate accomplishment

One can argue for a same-sex relationship
Because just like every relationship
The primary motivation is love
However, not every love is God
In the process of seeking God
One can find love, His way

*"You shall not lie [intimately] with a male as one lies with
a female; it is repulsive." Leviticus 18:22, AMP*

WiFi

The Holy Spirit

A virtual version of God

For an electronic generation

"But the Helper (Comforter, Advocate, Intercessor—Counselor, Strengthener, Standby), the Holy Spirit, whom the Father will send in My name [in My place, to represent Me and act on My behalf], He will teach you all things. And He will help you remember everything that I have told you." John 14:26, AMP

Harvest

I may be unsure how many single and available people there are to date
I may feel insecure during my time without a partner,
wondering if I am the problem
Doesn't make it right to break up another relationship
to satisfy my loneliness
Or to knowingly seduce a committed partner with the excuse,
"if only they met me first"

I may be unsure about my chances of winning a political appointment
Anxious that my supporters will succumb to another
Heavily bidding to purchase their loyalty
Doesn't make it right to commit a crime against another candidate
Forcing the hands of fate in my favor

A decision to take a selfish path
Is me opting to become someone else's negative prayer point
Is me choosing to be a reason why someone cries to God
By doing so, I put myself on the line

God is a just God
No matter how many sparks the relationship brings to me
Or how many coins the political appointment adds to my hoard
He wouldn't hesitate to discipline me
For stealing an opportunity that was never mine

While I dance in excitement
And throw a celebration party
Because what I stole in secret
Is finally mine in the open

I'd need to remember that judgment comes
From the One who sees both in secret and in the open
If I manage to skip out on a curse
I'll have to pray hard for my children

Because the treasure I stole
That made someone lose sleep
I will struggle wide awake to keep

"For they sow the wind [in evil]; And they reap the whirlwind [in disaster]." Hosea 8:7a, AMP

Overseer

Without a people, there is no president

Without staff, there is no manager

Without servants, there is no master

Yet He walked alone

As King all by Himself

Defying all the odds

Breaking all the rules

No servants, no staff, no people

No appointments, no elections, no opinions

Just God

Still God

God alone

"In the beginning, God (Elohim) created [by forming from nothing] the heavens and the earth. The earth was formless and void or a waste and emptiness, and darkness was upon the face of the deep [primeval ocean that covered the unformed earth]. The Spirit of God was moving (hovering, brooding) over the face of the waters." Genesis 1:1–2, AMP

Unique

Although we are cut from the same cloth

He created us beautifully different

In shape, mindset, exposure, and size

But society could manipulate our wills to become universal

So that we'll look, think, sound, and react alike

Such that a certain body type becomes the goal

A specific accent preferred

A certain status exalted

A country more desirable or another never enough

We chase irrelevant goals

With possessions we don't truly own

To impress people who don't contribute to our purpose

The yardstick He'll use to judge

Does not measure the similarities in our body shape, color, or status

But the fulfillment of the different purposes He has gifted each one

In our righteousness and obedience

"Don't copy the behavior and customs of this world, but let God transform you into a new person by changing the way you think. Then you will learn to know God's will for you, which is good and pleasing and perfect." Romans 12:2, NLT

Free Access

Communion is such a big deal to Him

So, He brought it to my feet

By tearing the veil of separation

Between the Holy of Holies and the rest of the temple

Equal access was given to the most religious person and to the least

No sacrificial lambs to slaughter

No temples to travel to

Just a mention of His name, Jesus

In any location, at any time, and we have full access to Him

Thank You Father for making it easy

I would never have been able to afford those lambs

My feet would have hardened on the mile-long trips to the temples

"Therefore, let us [with privilege] approach the throne of grace [that is, the throne of God's gracious favor] with confidence and without fear, so that we may receive mercy [for our failures] and find [His amazing] grace to help in time of need [an appropriate blessing, coming just at the right moment]." Hebrews 4:16, AMP

Qualifying Praises

He is the great Provider

Not just a provider

He is the good Shepherd

Not just a shepherd

Because when You provide money from the mouth of a fish

When You turn water into the best wine at a wedding

When You multiply food meant for one to feed thousands

When You empower a human to outrun chariots

There really should be none besides You

Anyone trying to compete falls to their death

There is absolutely no comparison

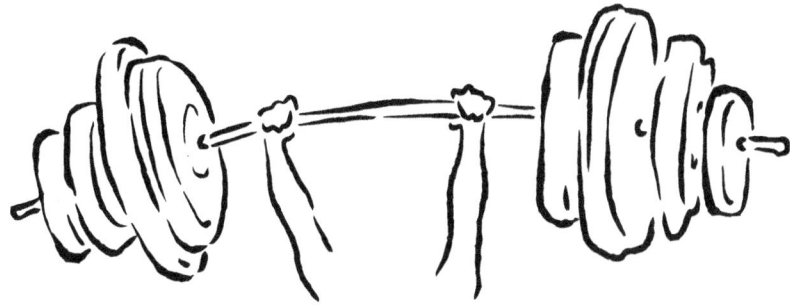

"Now to Him who is able to [carry out His purpose and] do superabundantly more than all that we dare ask or think [infinitely beyond our greatest prayers, hopes, or dreams], according to His power that is at work within us," Ephesians 3:20, AMP

Storm

He told me He was my cover

And then the rains drenched me

Of what purpose is a cover if I still get drenched by the rain?

After the fact, I understood the purpose of the rain

He showed me how He preserved me

From all the things that could have broken me during the storm

My idea of His covering was to prevent the storm

His definition of a covering was protection over what would have killed me

His focus was the salvation of another through my experience

Because He will never give me much more than I'm able to carry

The sharing of my rain-soaking testimony

Helped someone find salvation in Christ

"No temptation [regardless of its source] has overtaken or enticed you that is not common to human experience [nor is any temptation unusual or beyond human resistance]; but God is faithful [to His word—He is compassionate and trustworthy], and He will not let you be tempted beyond your ability [to resist], but along with the temptation He [has in the past and is now and] will [always] provide the way out as well, so that you will be able to endure it [without yielding, and will overcome temptation with joy]." 1 Corinthians 10:13, AMP

Love Choices

The audacity

To request to be loved

From a mortal I truly don't know

In ways I haven't yet loved myself

Yet He offers a love I didn't know I needed

In ways I never deserved

Surpassing every other type of love

A love He has made available

To the just and unjust

The diligent and unscrupulous

The saved and unsaved

A love He has made available to all

"And I am convinced that nothing can ever separate us from God's love. Neither death nor life, neither angels nor demons, neither our fears for today nor our worries about tomorrow—not even the powers of hell can separate us from God's love. No power in the sky above or in the earth below—indeed, nothing in all creation will ever be able to separate us from the love of God that is revealed in Christ Jesus our Lord." Romans 8:38–39, NLT

Unkind

I used to pray for my network to include the affluent and influential

So that when push comes to shove

They would come through for me

Until I was surrounded by friends rich but unkind

And I never felt more broke

A special kind of betrayal that pierced my heart

Knowing they had more than enough to help

But didn't choose me

When someone is kind to you

Whether they are rich, middle class, or poor

You feel heard, seen, and understood

They'll give their heart, bank, valuable advice, or a connection

Because they care enough

Pray you are never in a situation

Where you need something

from someone you've genuinely been selfless toward

Whom you hold in high esteem and who can help you

But chooses not to

"Two are better than one because they have a more satisfying return for their labor;for if either of them falls, the one will lift up his companion. But woe to him who is alone when he falls and does not have another to lift him up." Ecclesiastes 4:9-10, AMP

Proud Humility

I loved that I was humble
Couldn't be prouder
Humility is a quality sought by God Himself
The lack of it made Lucifer lose his position

Until the Holy Spirit chastised me
"You're no different from the proud"

My error was in the pride
That lay in my claim for humility

*"Everyone who is proud and arrogant in heart is disgusting
and exceedingly offensive to the Lord; Be assured he will
not go unpunished." Proverbs 16:5, AMP*

Testing Hypotheses

I'm not scared for the curious atheist
I am terrified for the atheist who refuses to seek

There should be no fears when you know that what you believe is the truth
That's why the three Hebrew friends said in the book of Daniel 3
"Even if God chooses not to save us, we will not bow to the golden image"
They were not only confident in God's ability to save
But in the choices that He makes
He is known to come through
But if He chooses not to
Then it is for the greater good

I challenge every atheist to seek
Seek earnestly, because you will find

"Ask and keep on asking and it will be given to you; seek and keep on seeking and you will find; knock and keep on knocking and the door will be opened to you." Matthew 7:7, AMP

Order

He has impeccable memory

But He chooses to wipe away our sins

A choice to forgive and forget

I ask myself why I have to go through consequences

Since He already forgave

He reminded me that He is a God of order

He meant it when He said, *"Give to Caesar what belongs to Caesar"*

If I broke a Caesarean law which had consequences

Then punishment will follow

If I break God's law

He again will choose

Whether to punish me Himself

Or use a "Caesar" to enforce the consequence of my behavior

It's a better choice to fall into His hands

Because He is kind, and when He forgives, He truly forgets

But with Caesar, you'll never know

"David said to Gad, 'I am in deep distress. Let me fall into the hands of the Lord, for his mercy is very great; but do not let me fall into human hands.' So the Lord sent a plague on Israel, and seventy thousand men of Israel fell dead. And God sent an angel to destroy Jerusalem. But as the angel was doing so, the Lord saw it and relented concerning the disaster and said to the angel who was destroying the people, 'Enough! Withdraw your hand.'" 1 Chronicles 21:13–15a, NIV

Hard Work

Some succeed at repurposing what would make life easier for others
Processing raw materials into finished valuable products
Money is a universal reward for providing value
A few pennies of sale, here and there, from billions of people
Soon enough, the innovator is now a "millionaire", "business mogul"

While I hope to be connected to someone
Whose family line has figured out the desires of people
And are now swimming in gold coins for it
I should intentionally spend time thinking of ways I can provide value
Because one thing is sure
People always need something to spend their money on

If I can figure out what they need
And ask God to glorify the works of my hand, that He may be glorified
I too can offer value and be rewarded for it

"If anyone is not willing to work, then he is not to eat, either. Indeed, we hear that some among you are leading an undisciplined and inappropriate life, doing no work at all, but acting like busybodies [meddling in other people's business]." 2 Thessalonians 3:10b–11, AMP

Audacious

What cannot kill me
Knows to whom I belong

How can someone think they can starve
The one whom the Lord feeds?

"Then the angel of the Lord came again a second time and touched him and said, 'Get up, and eat, for the journey is too long for you [without adequate sustenance].' So he got up and ate and drank, and with the strength of that food he traveled forty days and nights to Horeb (Sinai), the mountain of God." 1 Kings 19:7–8, AMP

Decisions

I was hurt

So, I prayed for vengeance to God

They later became remorseful

And prayed for repentance to the same God

Whose prayer do you think our God of love will answer?

"Jonah began by going a day's journey into the city, proclaiming, 'Forty more days and Nineveh will be overthrown.' The Ninevites believed God. A fast was proclaimed, and all of them, from the greatest to the least, put on sackcloth. When Jonah's warning reached the king of Nineveh, he rose from his throne, took off his royal robes, covered himself with sackcloth and sat down in the dust. This is the proclamation he issued in Nineveh: 'By the decree of the king and his nobles: Do not let people or animals, herds or flocks, taste anything; do not let them eat or drink. But let people and animals be covered with sackcloth. Let everyone call urgently on God. Let them give up their evil ways and their violence. Who knows? God may yet relent and with compassion turn from his fierce anger so that we will not perish.' When God saw what they did and how they turned from their evil ways, he relented and did not bring on them the destruction he had threatened." Jonah 3:4–10, NIV

Prisoned

Forgiveness frees the prisoner

It was only after I had forgiven

I realized the prisoner was me

"For if you forgive others their trespasses [their reckless and willful sins], your heavenly Father will also forgive you." Matthew 6:14, AMP

Choose Me

When Goodness and Mercy come to You

Seeking whom to follow

I pray You find me

I hope You choose me

I pray You favor me

*"For if you forgive others their trespasses [their reckless and willful sins],
your heavenly Father will also forgive you." Matthew 6:14, AMP*

Imperfectly Perfect

The sounds from my broken guitar strings aren't perfect
My words aren't melodious
But He listens to them anyway
And dances to my archaic tunes

I would continue to play only if He would listen
I'll dance only if He would dance with me

Minutes with Him
Is better than a lifetime without

Every moment with Him is memorable
And the best part about Him is
His children will always be number one

"For a day in Your courts is better than a thousand [anywhere else]; I would rather stand [as a doorkeeper] at the threshold of the house of my God than to live [at ease] in the tents of wickedness." Psalm 84:10, AMP

Untrained Soldier

I wonder why my breakthrough is trapped
in the self-discipline I keep avoiding
It would help if I understood that God loves me too much
To hand me a flaming sword for battle
Knowing I slept through my war training classes

I barely know how to run, fight, or hold a shield
I think it's too much to have a personal fast at least once every 1–2 weeks
I don't think it's necessary to wake up at night to pray
or to take a prayer walk
I cannot remember the last time I studied the Bible on my own
I barely recognize the voice of my Commander

Jesus spent three years training His disciples
before power was released to them
One thousand and ninety-five days of intense training
Do you think you can restfully snore your way to power?

Intentionally train yourself as a soldier of Christ
Practice self-discipline, make time to study, and pray

"A final word: Be strong in the Lord and in his mighty power. Put on all of God's armor so that you will be able to stand firm against all strategies of the devil. For we are not fighting against flesh-and-blood enemies, but against evil rulers and authorities of the unseen world, against mighty powers in this dark world, and against evil spirits in the heavenly places." Ephesians 6:10–12, NLT

Battery Life

I deceive myself into thinking I'm still young
When I have no control over time

If according to God's schedule, my life span is supposed to be 35 years
And I'm currently 30, then I'm pretty old
With less than 15% left on my life battery

If my life span is supposed to be 75 years
And I'm currently 30, then I'm about middle-aged
With over 50% left on my life battery

What would be best is to know my time of death
However, without the luxury of such information
While I pray for a long life, I should pray to fulfill my purpose without delay
And become intentional about accomplishing it
Before my battery fades and is out

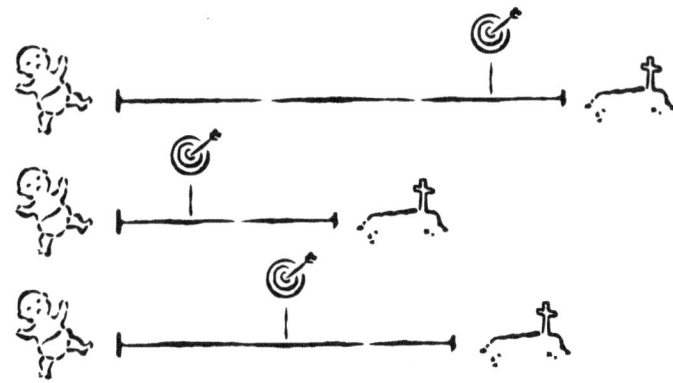

*"But my life is worth nothing to me unless I use it for finishing the work
assigned me by the Lord Jesus—the work of telling others the Good
News about the wonderful grace of God." Acts 20:24, NLT*

Will

My will is mine, and His will is His
I was created in His image and likeness
I have the mind of Christ

If I set my mind on holy and righteous things
I'm acting out the mind of God
So then, my mind is His mind
My will is His will and His, mine

One stitch at a time
He has interwoven our wills
Such that one couldn't exist without the other
And when I think out of His will, His Spirit pricks me like a needle
So, I know when I'm weaving an independent path

As long as I remain in right standing
My will remains His will
His will is that I make heaven with as many souls as possible
While in that pursuit, He said to ask anything in His name and He will do it
So, anything that makes me comfortable and happy
while in right standing, is His will

Therefore, ask away

"If you ask Me anything in My name [as My representative], I will do it." John 14:14, AMP

Talkative

I love my friends
Maybe a little too much
When I need advice or a listening ear
There is always someone with experience
To help fill the gaps in my silence

The Holy spirit asked me, *"did I ask you to share that?"*
The Bible says Mary kept these things in her heart – Luke 2:19
"Have you prayed about your situation
as much as you have chatted about it?"

"Trust in and rely confidently on the Lord with all your heart and do not rely on your own insight or understanding. In all your ways know and acknowledge and recognize Him, and He will make your paths straight and smooth [removing obstacles that block your way]." Proverbs 3:5–6, AMP

Glass Ceilings

Beautiful architecture

Full access to see the weather in its most natural form

Direct sunlight with a choice to get a tan or to seek shade

Enjoying rainfall without getting soaked

Watching the snow freeze the earth as my heater provides me with comfort

With glass ceilings, I can see heaven and choose not to be affected

I can watch miracles happen but the glass barrier hinders access

I'm aware of His power, I see it work, but I can be unchanged

If a stone breaks through the glass ceiling

Such that I see the rain and feel its drops

I see the snow and freeze in it

Then I'd experience Him, His power, His promises, and understand His ways

Most Christians prefer to live under glass ceilings

Preaching to other people about a God they haven't personally encountered

Speaking in tongues they don't get lost in

If He were to break the glass

Would you be able to withstand the real Him?

"When the day of Pentecost had come, they were all together in one place, and suddenly a sound came from heaven like a rushing violent wind, and it filled the whole house where they were sitting. There appeared to them tongues resembling fire, which were being distributed [among them], and they rested on each one of them [as each person received the Holy Spirit]. And they were all filled [that is, diffused throughout their being] with the Holy Spirit and began to speak in othertongues (different languages), as the Spirit was giving them the ability to speak out [clearly and appropriately]." Acts 2:1-4, AMP

Trust

I was fond of saying

My friend will never do this to me

Until I was asked in my spirit, *"What makes you so confident?"*

Not God coming for my total dependence on fallible humanity

Except my confidence was not in them

My trust was in God

That He will not allow detrimental arrows concealed in "love"

To pierce through my heart

"As for you, you meant evil against me, but God meant it for good in order to bring about this present outcome, that many people would be kept alive [as they are this day]." Genesis 50:20, AMP

Savior

I hope I always feel small when I'm next to You
Never to take You for granted

You, the only one qualified to throw a stone, didn't
No other hero could provide the kind of saving I needed ·

"And they said to Him, 'Teacher, this woman has been caught in the very
act of adultery. Now in the Law Moses commanded us to stone such women
[to death]. So, what do You say [to do with her—what is Your sentence]?' They
said this to test Him, hoping that they would have grounds for accusing Him.
But Jesus stooped down and began writing on the ground with His finger.
However, when they persisted in questioning Him, He straightened up and
said, 'He who is without [any] sin among you, let him be the first to throw
a stone at her.'" John 8:4–7, AMP

Vessel

He was generous enough to give me life and other amenities
I'm a beneficiary of his generosity

So, if He asks me to pour His gift to me into others
Sacrificing a little of my time or resources
Who am I to say no?

"Now in a large house there are not only vessels and objects of gold and silver, but also vessels of wood and of earthenware, and some are for honorable (noble, good) use and some for dishonorable (ignoble, common). Therefore, if anyone cleanses himself from these things [which are dishonorable—disobedient, sinful], he will be a vessel for honor, sanctified [set apart for a special purpose and], useful to the Master, prepared for every good work." 2 Timothy 2:20–21, AMP

Gift

The greatest gift of all

Wasn't wrapped and placed under a well-decorated tree

He was beaten and nailed to a cross

"Have this same attitude in yourselves which was in Christ Jesus [look to Him as your example in selfless humility], who, although He existed in the form and unchanging essence of God [as One with Him, possessing the fullness of all the divine attributes—the entire nature of deity], did not regard equality with God a thing to be grasped or asserted [as if He did not already possess it, or was afraid of losing it]; but emptied Himself [without renouncing or diminishing His deity, but only temporarily giving up the outward expression of divine equality and His rightful dignity] by assuming the form of a bond-servant, and being made in the likeness of men [He became completely human but was without sin, being fully God and fully man]. After He was found in [terms of His] outward appearance as a man [for a divinely-appointed time], He humbled Himself [still further] by becoming obedient [to the Father] to the point of death, even death on a cross." Philippians 2:5-8, AMP

Fe-male

Don't ever doubt your capacity
Don't ever doubt your gifting
You're much more special than the stars in the sky

God is a God of order
Although He is capable of overriding His laws
He allows order so that there is pattern and predictability for His people
Like the order of baby creation, sperm + egg = fetus

Although "order" would be to follow the same pattern to create baby Jesus
He skipped over the use of sperm
He did not need the male
But He needed the female
He needed her baking oven, her uterus

Whenever you feel less than human
Remember that when God was to choose the first home
for the only Savior
He chose your oven

Remember that God overrode the male
But couldn't do life without you

"For God said to Moses, 'I will show mercy to anyone I choose, and I will show compassion to anyone I choose.' So, it is God who decides to show mercy. We can neither choose it nor work for it." Romans 9:15–16, NLT

Flee

Avoid all appearances of evil

The devil takes much more than he gives

Imagine giving Eve a fruit

And taking away easy access to God's presence in the Garden of Eden

"Abstain from every form of evil [withdraw and keep away from it]." Thessalonians 5:22, AMP

Copy Paste

I was so worried about being left behind

Everyone was running

So, I picked up my pace and followed suit

Only thing was

I hadn't asked myself

If I was running in the direction of my purpose

"Therefore, I do not run without a definite goal; I do not flail around like one beating the air [just shadow boxing]." 1 Corinthians 9:26, AMP

Another Fall

Life circumstances became so distracting
I had fallen out of love with Him several times
Fortunately, His Spirit had already fallen for me

His eyes watch me
He is my glory
The lifter of my head

*"And lo, I am with you always [remaining with you perpetually
—regardless of circumstance, and on every occasion],
even to the end of the age." Matthew 28:20b, AMP*

As I Am

He is inexhaustible

A good Provider to all His children

I used to wonder why some were wealthier, more confident, smarter

I look in the mirror and ask myself where I was in heaven

when these qualities were being allocated

Then He said

"It's okay to admire someone else's beauty without questioning your own"

The light from a diamond shouldn't detract from that of a sapphire

"God saw everything that He had made, and behold, it was very good and He validated it completely." Genesis 1:31a, AMP

None Left Behind

Christian artists may produce a million albums
And draw souls to Christ
But amid the crowd, there are still a few
Who will get saved only on the condition that
Their favorite secular artist received salvation

Pray for secular artists
Just as much as you would for Christian artists
Pray for the ones who pull traffic on several streams
Pray for those who have amassed fame and affluence
And have been given a respected voice of influence

So that when their hearts become set on fire for Jesus
Their baby steps into Christ's kingdom
Will pull millions of souls with them

*"Therefore, confess your sins to one another [your false
steps, your offenses], and pray for one another, that you may
be healed and restored. The heartfelt and persistent prayer of
a righteous man (believer) can accomplish much [when put
into action and made effective by God—it is dynamic and
can have tremendous power]." James 5:16, AMP*

Journey

He has us arranged in a line

And we are unsure of who goes first or who comes next

Uninformed of when it'll be my turn to cross the lines of death

Or the turn of someone close to me

Unable to get a sneak peek of the other side, from someone already there

So much uncertainty

With one assurance - we'll all leave the earth, sometime

While I wait

I'll light up the lives of those around me

I'll put smiles on the faces of those who mourn

I'll be generous and compassionate

I'll work to create wealth for generations unborn

I'll enjoy life and leave a good legacy

When I get to the front

I'll leave with no regrets

No love unshared

No praises unsung

No hate pondered upon

I'll leave peacefully and freely

Ready for another journey

"So teach us to number our days, that we may cultivate and bring to You a heart of wisdom." Psalm 90:12, AMP

Flowers

I don't want to wait until I'm old and gray to give You flowers
I want to give You flowers in my daily walk with You
Through my daily worship to You

I want to give You flowers in the ways I hold You in the highest regard
Through my shameless conviction that You're the only true Savior

I want to give You flowers in the way I long to spend time with You
In my flawed attempts to always do right by You

I want to give You flowers in the way my presence brings You joy
In the way I've learned generosity and kindness because of You

I want to give You flowers while I still have teeth, thick hair, and tight skin
So that when my teeth fall
My skin wrinkles
My full locks turn sparse and sparkly
I would have shown You how much I love You
And would have decorated Your space
With the best of flowers, that only years in Your presence could buy

"So teach us to number our days, that we may cultivate and bring to You a heart of wisdom." Psalm 90:12, AMP

Familiarity

I want to walk into heaven
And recognize Your face

I want to walk by You
And have You recollect Your favorite parts of our many discussions on earth

I want to see Your face
And feel like I've known You all my life

"Blessed [anticipating God's presence, spiritually mature] are the pure in heart [those with integrity, moral courage, and godly character], for they will see God." Matthew 5:8, AMP

A Call to Jesus

Jesus came to seek and save you and me
He desires to have a relationship with us
He only asks that we seek to be saved by Him
If these words resonate with you, I'd like you to say this prayer with me:

Dear Lord Jesus,
I need you
Thank you for dying on the cross for me
I invite You into my heart
And accept you as my Savior and Lord
Take control of my life
Make me the person You created me to be
In Jesus Name, **AMEN!**

If you said this prayer, I'm honored to welcome you to the best family
Where we pray to live righteously by His grace
as we await the return of Jesus Christ
The Bible says the angels rejoice when a soul is saved
So, I'm confident that there is rejoicing in heaven
just because of your salvation
I encourage you to join a bible believing church to help you grow in Him

May the Lord bless you and keep you!
May the Lord make His face shine upon you and be gracious to you!
May the Lord turn His face toward you and give you peace
In Jesus Name, **AMEN!**

I love you and I'm rooting for you!

"For God so loved the world, that He gave His only begotten Son, that whosoever believeth in Him should not perish, but have everlasting life." John 3:16, KJV

REFLECTION

_____

_____

_____

_____

_____

_____

_____

_____

_____

_____

_____

_____

_____

_____

_____

_____

_____

_____

_____

_____

_____

_____

_____

_____

_____

_____

_____

_____

_____

www.ingramcontent.com/pod-product-compliance
Lightning Source LLC
Chambersburg PA
CBHW051316120626
46547CB00015B/2269